W9-AWG-752

COTTONTAILS
LITTLE RABBITS
OF FIELD AND FOREST

by Ron Fisher

Ears alert, a cottontail watches for danger.

BOOKS FOR YOUNG EXPLORERS
NATIONAL GEOGRAPHIC SOCIETY

Copyright © 1989 National Geographic Society   Library of Congress CIP Data: p. 32

 The sun is shining, and the day is fine. The meadow is warm and dry. The grass is sweet. A rabbit leaps so high and far it is almost flying. This rabbit's tail looks like a ball of cotton. So it is called a cottontail rabbit.

There are about 14 kinds of cottontails. Each has a different name. This desert cottontail is standing on its hind legs to look around. Maybe it is looking for something to eat. Maybe it is looking for danger. Maybe it is looking for other cottontails.

Baby eastern cottontails sleep in their nest. They are about seven days old. Baby rabbits are called kittens. Will they grow up to be cats?

A mountain cottontail is gathering grass.
She is building a nest for her young. She will dig
a small hole, then line it with grass and
with soft fur that she pulls from her body.

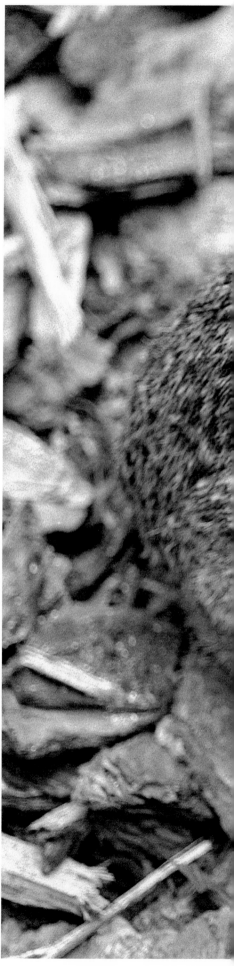

Cottontail kittens cuddle in a soft pile.
Soon their mother will come feed them.
Cottontail mothers are called does.
Fathers are called bucks.

A doe holds very still so a young cottontail
can drink her milk. She may feed her kittens
early in the morning and late in the evening.
She comes to the nest and uncovers the babies.
She stands above them while they nurse.
Then she covers the nest with grass to hide it.

 Kittens that are old enough to leave the nest are called juveniles. They start exploring on their own when they are about two weeks old.

It is an exciting new world to young cottontails. They see new sights and try new things. They sniff new smells and they taste new tastes. Ripe, squishy, juicy, fresh blackberries are a tasty treat to a juvenile cottontail.

A bed of green leaves
is like a jungle
to a young cottontail.
In a field of tall grass,
a juvenile rabbit finds a
hidden place for a rest.

A marsh rabbit stands on its hind legs. It uses its eyes to look for danger. It uses its nose to sniff for danger. What does it use to listen for danger?

A cottontail's eyes are on the sides of its head. It can see to the left and to the right and in front and behind. A cottontail has big ears. It can move them up and down and almost all the way around. It can hear an enemy before the enemy sees it.

Hippety-hop. This is the way a cottontail makes tracks. Powerful hind legs help a rabbit leap in the snow. A rabbit running fast could leap clear across your driveway.

The cottontail that made these tracks was hopping quickly in a straight line. If something is chasing it, a cottontail will zigzag. Almost all dogs can run faster than cottontails.

 If something frightens a rabbit, it may "freeze."
It will be very still and quiet until the danger passes.
This rabbit is frozen. But does that mean it is cold?

Most cottontails don't have special homes. They sit down wherever they want—even at a prairie dog's front door.

A rabbit on a big rock can see enemies. Rabbits usually sit still during the day and explore and eat at night.

A cave is a safe place for a rest. This rabbit's eyes are open, and its ears are up. It is alert.

 This rabbit is using its paw to dig a shallow place to rest in the dirt. The resting place is called a form. It just fits the rabbit's body.

One cottontail made its form in some pine needles near a log. Another made its form in the snow. Resting rabbits tuck in their legs and lower their ears.

CHOMP, CHOMP, MUNCH, MUNCH.
A cottontail has big, sharp teeth.
It gets a bite of grass with its front teeth.
It grinds up the grass with its back teeth.

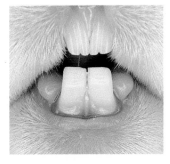

Wild rabbits eat grass, clover, lettuce, and
carrots; dandelions, willows, cherries,
blueberries, blackberries, and bushes.
When a rabbit chews, its nose wiggles.

Rabbits on tiptoe reach for tender young leaves growing on bushes.

A hungry rabbit stretches way out for some fresh grass. When it has eaten all it can reach, it will bring its hind feet forward with a . . . HOP!

When winter comes, cottontails make pathways under snow-covered bushes. Sometimes they dig down through the snow to find food. Sometimes they lick the snow to get a drink.

 Rabbits wash after eating, just as people do.
A rabbit can wash almost every part of its body.
It wets its paws, then uses them like a washcloth.

It washes its ears, its nose, its sides, its feet.
It even washes between its toes!
Rabbits spend almost as much time washing as eating.

A desert cottontail comes to a pool of water to drink. Rabbits usually don't need to drink water. They get almost all they need from grasses and other plants they eat.

Another rabbit rolls in the dust to get rid of ticks and fleas.

Is this one rabbit resting, or two, or three? How many ears do you see?

A cottontail finds a shady spot on a hot day. Lying with its belly flat on the ground may help the rabbit cool off.

Even if you live in a city, you may see cottontails. They may be in your park or garden. They may nibble your grass.

Wild Rabbits

All cottontails are rabbits, but not all rabbits are cottontails.
There are many other kinds of rabbits. Some are called hares.
Rabbits live almost everywhere in the United States and
in nearly every other country in the world.

Ryukyu Rabbit - Japan

European Rabbit - Worldwide

Bushman Hare - South Africa

Hispid Hare - Asia

Volcano Rabbit - Mexico

Red Rock Rabbit - Africa

Domestic Rabbits

Many people keep domestic rabbits as pets. Some domestic rabbits are raised to win prizes at shows, like dogs or cats.

Domestic rabbits of all sizes come from the wild European rabbit. Travis Reed holds the smallest and largest breeds of domestic rabbit. The Siamese Sable Netherland Dwarf weighs 2 pounds. The Light Gray Flemish Giant weighs 16 pounds.

Some domestic rabbits have floppy ears. Some have spots or stripes.

Black Harlequin (Japanese)

Broken Tortoise English Lop

Black English Spot

Belgian Hare

Blue Rex

Florida White

Black Dutch

Solid Steel French Lop

Black Checkered Giant

White English Angora

Dwarf Hotot

Broken Agouti Mini Lop

Published by

The National Geographic Society, Washington, D. C.
Gilbert M. Grosvenor, *President and Chairman of the Board*
Melvin M. Payne, Thomas W. McKnew, *Chairmen Emeritus*
Owen R. Anderson, *Executive Vice President*
Robert L. Breeden, *Senior Vice President,*
 Publications and Educational Media

Prepared by

The Special Publications and School Services Division
Donald J. Crump, *Director*
Philip B. Silcott, *Associate Director*
Bonnie S. Lawrence, *Assistant Director*

Staff for this book

Jane H. Buxton, *Managing Editor*
Debra A. Antonini, *Picture Editor and Researcher*
John G. Agnone, *Consulting Illustrations Editor*
Louise Ponsford, *Art Director*
Annie Lunsford, *Artist*
Sharon Kocsis Berry, *Illustrations Assistant*
Catherine G. Cruz, Marisa J. Farabelli, Lisa A. LaFuria,
 Sandra F. Lotterman, Eliza C. Morton, Dru McLoud
 Stancampiano, *Staff Assistants*

Engraving, Printing, and Product Manufacture

George V. White, *Director;* Vincent P. Ryan and George J.
 Zeller, Jr., *Managers, Manufacturing and Quality Management*
David V. Showers, *Production Manager*
Kathleen M. Cirucci, *Production Project Manager*
Carol R. Curtis, *Senior Production Staff Assistant*

Consultants

Dr. Joseph A. Chapman, Department of Fisheries and Wildlife,
 Utah State University, *Scientific Consultant*
Susan W. Altemus, *Educational Consultant*
Dr. Lynda Bush, *Reading Consultant*

The Society is grateful to the following individuals for their
generous assistance during the preparation of this book: Winn
Jones, LaPlata, Maryland; Paul and Barbara Munro, Bryans
Road, Maryland; and Owen Yates, Mechanicsville, Virginia.

In winter, a mountain cottontail wears
a thick coat that keeps it warm.
Big furry feet help it walk on snow.

COVER: In summer, a little rabbit sits
among bright dandelion blossoms.
The cottontail is about a month old.

Illustrations Credits

Alvin E. Staffan (cover); Brian Milne/FIRST LIGHT ASSOCIATED PHOTOGRAPHERS (1); Tom McHugh/PHOTO RESEARCHERS, INC. (2 left); N.G.S. Photographer Bates Littlehales (2-3); Esther Schmidt/VALAN PHOTOS (4 left); Jack Dermid (4-5); Tom J. Ulrich (6 left, 21 lower, 22); John P. Solum (6-7); ANIMALS ANIMALS/Robert A. Lubeck (8); Art Wolfe (9 upper); © Tom & Pat Leeson (9 lower, 23 lower); Erwin & Peggy Bauer/BRUCE COLEMAN LTD. (10 upper); C. Allan Morgan (10 lower); William J. Weber (11); Tom Brakefield (12 upper left and upper right, 13 all); John Serrao (12 lower); Alan Blank/BRUCE COLEMAN INC. (14-15); John Shaw/BRUCE COLEMAN LTD. (15 upper left); Franz J. Camenzind (15 upper right, 23 upper left); Wilf Schurig (15 lower right); Wayne Lankinen (16-17); Robert Pollock (17 upper and lower, 21 upper right); Wyman Meinzer (18, 19 lower left and lower right, 23 upper center and upper right); Michael Bourque/VALAN PHOTOS (19 upper); Gary R. Zahm (20 lower left); Dennis W. Schmidt/VALAN PHOTOS (20-21); © Thomas Wiewandt (24); Leonard Lee Rue III (25 upper); Jim Brandenburg (25 lower); Rod Planck/TOM STACK & ASSOCIATES (26-27); NATURE PRODUCTION (28 upper left); Jane Burton/BRUCE COLEMAN LTD. (28 upper right, 30 upper left, 30 center left and center right, 31 center right); Anthony Bannister/ANTHONY BANNISTER LIBRARY (28 lower right); COMSTOCK/George D. Lepp (28 lower center); Joanna Van Gruisen/SURVIVAL ANGLIA (28 lower left); A. Duthie/ANTHONY BANNISTER LIBRARY (28 center left); N.G.S. Photographer Joseph H. Bailey (29); Jane Burton/BRUCE COLEMAN INC. (30 upper right and lower left, 31 upper left and upper right); Norvia Behling (30 lower right, 31 center left, 31 lower left and lower right); Frank R. Martin/PHOTO RESEARCHERS, INC. (32).

Library of Congress CIP Data
Fisher, Ronald M.
 Cottontails : little rabbits of field and forest / by Ron Fisher.
  p. cm. — Books for young explorers
 Bibliography: p.
 Summary: Illustrates how the cottontail rabbit explores its environment, eats, washes, senses danger, rests, and cares for its young. Also describes wild and domestic rabbits around the world.
 ISBN 0-87044-769-6 (regular edition)
 ISBN 0-87044-774-2 (library edition)
 1. Cottontails—Juvenile literature. [1. Cottontails.
2. Rabbits.] I. Title. II. Series.
QL737.L32F57 1989
599.32'2—dc20   89-3316
                                                   CIP
                                                   AC

More About COTTONTAILS
Little Rabbits of Field and Forest

This bold cottontail may get in trouble. Rabbits that come into backyards and gardens to eat flowers and vegetables are pests. Some people put up fences to try to keep them out. Rabbits that live at the edges of farmers' fields can badly damage such crops as wheat and corn when feeding on them in the spring.

Rabbits are among the most common and recognizable animals on earth. There are about 25 species of wild rabbits, and more than half of the species are cottontails. They live on every continent except Antarctica.

The closest relatives of rabbits are pikas and hares. Rabbits, pikas, and hares live in mountains, swamps, marshes, rain forests, and deserts, as well as on grasslands and tundra.

Smaller than their relatives, pikas are mouselike animals that live in western North America, in southeastern Europe, and in parts of Asia. Hares, like rabbits, are found on every continent except Antarctica.

Some people confuse rabbits and hares. Hares look like rabbits, but are usually larger. The hind legs and ears of hares are longer than those of rabbits. Even the names are sometimes confusing. The jackrabbit and the snowshoe rabbit are hares, and the Belgian hare (30),* hispid hare (28), and bushman hare (28) are really rabbits.

Scientists group rabbits, pikas, and hares into an order of mammals called *Lagomorpha*. All lagomorphs use their sharp front teeth (19) to cut the many kinds of plants they eat. Like rodents, lagomorphs have front teeth that grow throughout life. Unlike rodents, however, lagomorphs have two pairs of upper front teeth. One pair is located right behind the other. In all, rabbits and hares usually have 28 teeth; pikas have 26 teeth.

Rabbits, hares, and pikas all molt, or gradually shed their hair. Some molt once a year, others twice a year. The winter hair is coarser, longer, and thicker than the summer hair. In autumn, some North American hares molt and grow new white hair, which helps them hide in the snow. Rabbits and pikas do not grow a white coat.

Female rabbits are called does. Some cottontails begin reproducing at about three months. Cottontails produce several litters a year. One litter averages five kittens. A single doe may give birth to as many as 30 young each year.

In North America, most cottontails make shallow resting places called forms (16-17). Sometimes they borrow the abandoned burrows of other animals (15). One species of cottontail, the pygmy rabbit, builds its own burrow. The burrow may have two or more entrances, and the tunnels and chambers may extend three feet under the ground.

* Numbers in parentheses refer to pages in *Cottontails: Little Rabbits of Field and Forest.*

Unlike most North American cottontails, the wild European rabbit (28) digs a complex system of burrows called a warren. Groups of the rabbits live together in a warren, which has many openings. One warren that scientists studied held 407 rabbits and had 2,080 openings.

Lagomorphs have many enemies that hunt them on the ground: foxes, weasels, bobcats, coyotes, snakes, dogs, and badgers—as well as humans. Eagles, hawks, and owls swoop down from the sky to catch them for food.

times, however, it will "freeze," or sit very still (14-15). Its grayish or brownish coat acts as camouflage and blends in with its surroundings. At other times, a rabbit may swim to escape danger. Some rabbits, like the desert cottontail (1, 2, 10, 20-21, 22, 23, 24, 26-27) and the brush rabbit, may even climb a tree.

Life is difficult for rabbits, hares, and pikas. Despite their defenses, lagomorphs do not usually live long. They die either from predation or from disease. In the wild, rabbits survive for about a year. Some hares and

Domestic rabbits are soft and cuddly and can be handled safely. But if they are frightened or mishandled, they can inflict painful scratches and bites. Never pick up a rabbit by the ears. Using one hand, lift the rabbit by the fold of skin over its shoulders. At the same time, support the rabbit with your other hand.

A pet rabbit needs a clean, roomy cage—called a hutch—that provides plenty of fresh air but gives shelter from wind, rain, and too much sun. Pet rabbits need about one square foot of space per pound of rabbit. They also need plenty of clean water and nourishing food. Commercial brands of rabbit food sold by pet stores help supply a balanced diet.

Black-tailed jackrabbit

Pika

Eastern cottontail

Pikas, rabbits, and hares are members of the order of mammals called *Lagomorpha*. They look a little like mice, but are more closely related to deer. The black-tailed jackrabbit is a kind of hare.

Some rabbits and pikas act as guards that watch for danger while others of their kind eat. A watchdog rabbit will stand on its hind legs, and if it sees a threat, it will sound an alarm by thumping on the ground with its hind feet. Some pikas give warning calls that sound like sharp barks.

Rabbits have keen senses of hearing and smell, which help alert them to danger. Often, a rabbit will run when it senses danger (3, 12-13). Some-

pikas may live as long as five years in the wild.

Wild rabbits do not make good pets; they dislike being caged and may become sick and die if they are not cared for properly. Domestic rabbits (29-30), on the other hand, often make fine pets. They are bred to be tame. There are more than 50 breeds of domestic rabbits, with hundreds of varieties. They all descend from the wild European rabbit (28).

ADDITIONAL READING

Biography of a Cottontail, by Lucille Trost. (New York, G. P. Putnam's Sons, 1971). Ages 8-12.

Book of Mammals, 2 vols. (Washington, D.C., National Geographic Society, 1981). Ages 8 and up.

Cottontail, by Leonard Lee Rue III. (New York, Thomas Y. Crowell Co., 1965). Family reading.

Encyclopedia of Pet Rabbits, by David Robinson. (Neptune, N.J., TFH Publications, 1979). Family reading.

Rabbits, by Fiona Henrie. (London, Franklin Watts, 1980). Ages 7-12.

Rabbits, by Herbert S. Zim. (New York, William Morrow and Co., 1948). Ages 8-12.

Wild Animals of North America. (Washington, D.C., National Geographic Society, 1979). Family reading.